EMMANUEL JOSEPH

From Me to We, Creativity, Self-Compassion, and Decision-Making for Stronger Communities

Copyright © 2025 by Emmanuel Joseph

All rights reserved. No part of this publication may be reproduced, stored or transmitted in any form or by any means, electronic, mechanical, photocopying, recording, scanning, or otherwise without written permission from the publisher. It is illegal to copy this book, post it to a website, or distribute it by any other means without permission.

First edition

*This book was professionally typeset on Reedsy.
Find out more at reedsy.com*

Contents

1 Chapter 1   1
2 Chapter One: Creativity and Community   3
3 Chapter Two: Self-Compassion and Community   6
4 Chapter Three: Decision-Making and Community   9
5 Chapter Four: Building Stronger Communities   12
6 Chapter Five: Overcoming Challenges   15

1

Chapter 1

Introduction
Understanding the Power of Community

In a world that often celebrates individual achievements and personal success, the significance of community can sometimes fade into the background. Yet, it is within communities that we find our true strength, resilience, and support. The journey from "me" to "we" is not just a shift in mindset but a fundamental transformation that can lead to richer, more fulfilling lives.

Imagine a world where creativity flows not just from isolated individuals but from a collective pool of ideas and experiences. This chapter explores the profound impact that a shift from individualism to collectivism can have on our society. We will delve into the importance of fostering creativity, practicing self-compassion, and making decisions that benefit the greater good.

In our increasingly interconnected world, the boundaries that once separated us are dissolving. This interconnectedness offers a unique opportunity to build stronger, more vibrant communities. By embracing the principles of creativity, self-compassion, and collaborative decision-making, we can create a future where everyone thrives.

As we embark on this journey together, let us remember that the power of community lies not in its size but in the strength of its connections. When we come together with open hearts and minds, we unlock the potential to create lasting change. Welcome to the transformative journey from "me" to "we."

2

Chapter One: Creativity and Community

The Role of Creativity in Society

Creativity is not confined to the realms of art and literature; it permeates every aspect of our lives. From problem-solving to innovation, creative thinking is the driving force behind progress and development. In this chapter, we will explore how creativity can address communal challenges and bring about positive change.

Communities thrive when their members actively engage in creative pursuits. Whether it's finding innovative solutions to local issues or simply creating spaces for artistic expression, creativity fosters a sense of belonging and purpose. It encourages individuals to think outside the box and collaborate in ways that lead to groundbreaking discoveries.

One of the most powerful aspects of creativity is its ability to transcend barriers. It knows no boundaries and can unite people from diverse backgrounds. By harnessing the collective creative potential of a community, we can tackle even the most complex problems and find solutions that benefit everyone.

As we journey through this chapter, we will uncover the myriad ways in which creativity can enhance our communities. From inspiring new ideas to fostering a culture of innovation, creativity has the power to transform our world. Together, let us embrace the boundless possibilities that creativity offers and work towards building stronger, more resilient communities.

Fostering Collaborative Creativity

The magic of creativity is amplified when it is shared and nurtured within a collaborative environment. In this chapter, we will delve into the power of collaborative creativity and explore strategies to cultivate it within our communities.

When individuals come together to create, they bring with them a wealth of diverse perspectives and experiences. This diversity is the bedrock of innovation, as it allows for the cross-pollination of ideas and the emergence of new, exciting possibilities. Collaborative creativity not only enhances the quality of the final outcome but also strengthens the bonds between community members.

Successful collaborations often arise from a culture that values openness and mutual respect. By creating spaces where individuals feel safe to express their ideas and take risks, we can foster an environment that nurtures creativity. This chapter will highlight examples of successful collaborations and provide practical tips for fostering a collaborative spirit.

At the heart of collaborative creativity lies the belief that we are stronger together. By pooling our talents and working towards a common goal, we can achieve far more than we could individually. Let us explore the transformative power of collaboration and discover how we can harness it to build vibrant, dynamic communities.

Creativity as a Tool for Social Change

Art and creativity have always been powerful tools for advocacy and social justice. From murals that capture the spirit of a movement to literature that challenges the status quo, creative expression has driven societal progress throughout history. In this chapter, we will explore how creativity can be harnessed to promote social change and strengthen communities.

Communities often face complex issues that require innovative solutions. Creative approaches can provide fresh perspectives and inspire new ways of thinking. Whether through community art projects, theater performances, or public installations, creativity can engage and mobilize people, sparking conversations that lead to meaningful action.

One of the most compelling aspects of creativity is its ability to connect with people on an emotional level. Art has the power to evoke empathy and inspire individuals to take a stand. By tapping into the universal language of creativity, we can bridge divides and foster a sense of shared humanity.

As we navigate this chapter, we will examine historical and contemporary examples of how creative expression has fueled social change. We will also discuss practical ways to incorporate creativity into our advocacy efforts and build stronger, more resilient communities.

3

Chapter Two: Self-Compassion and Community

The Importance of Self-Compassion

Before we can care for others, we must learn to care for ourselves. Self-compassion is the foundation of personal well-being and a key component of community building. In this chapter, we will explore the concept of self-compassion and its role in fostering healthier, more empathetic communities.

Self-compassion involves treating ourselves with the same kindness and understanding that we offer to others. It means recognizing our imperfections and acknowledging that we are all part of the shared human experience. When we practice self-compassion, we build a stronger sense of self-worth and resilience.

Communities are composed of individuals, and the well-being of each member contributes to the overall health of the community. By prioritizing self-compassion, we create a ripple effect that extends to those around us. When we are kind to ourselves, we are better equipped to extend that kindness to others.

Throughout this chapter, we will delve into the benefits of self-compassion and offer practical strategies for cultivating it in our daily lives. By embracing self-compassion, we can build stronger, more supportive communities that thrive on empathy and mutual respect.

Practicing Self-Compassion

Incorporating self-compassion into our lives requires intentional effort and practice. This chapter provides practical steps for developing a kinder relationship with ourselves and fostering a culture of self-compassion within our communities.

One of the first steps in practicing self-compassion is to become aware of our inner dialogue. Often, we are our harshest critics, but by recognizing and challenging negative self-talk, we can begin to treat ourselves with greater kindness. Mindfulness exercises and journaling can help us become more attuned to our thoughts and feelings.

Another important aspect of self-compassion is self-care. Taking time to nurture our physical, emotional, and mental well-being is essential for overall health. This chapter offers suggestions for self-care activities that can be easily integrated into our daily routines, such as meditation, exercise, and creative pursuits.

Self-compassion also involves setting healthy boundaries and recognizing our limits. By honoring our needs and giving ourselves permission to rest, we can prevent burnout and maintain our well-being. This chapter provides tips for setting boundaries and prioritizing self-care without guilt.

As we journey through this chapter, we will explore various exercises and reflections to help readers develop self-compassion. By practicing self-compassion, we can create a more supportive and empathetic community where everyone feels valued and cared for.

The Ripple Effect of Self-Compassion

When individuals practice self-compassion, it creates a ripple effect that can positively impact those around them. This chapter examines how self-compassionate individuals contribute to healthier, more empathetic communities and offers insights into how we can nurture this positive influence.

Self-compassion fosters emotional resilience, which enables individuals to navigate challenges with greater ease. When community members are emotionally resilient, they are better equipped to support one another during difficult times. This chapter explores the connection between self-compassion and emotional resilience, highlighting the benefits for both individuals and communities.

Furthermore, self-compassion promotes empathy and understanding. When we are kind to ourselves, we are more likely to extend that kindness to others. This chapter discusses the role of empathy in building strong communities and provides strategies for fostering empathetic interactions.

The ripple effect of self-compassion extends beyond individual interactions to influence the broader community. By creating a culture of self-compassion, we can cultivate an environment where everyone feels supported and valued. This chapter offers practical suggestions for promoting self-compassion within communities, such as organizing workshops, support groups, and community events.

As we explore the ripple effect of self-compassion, we will uncover the profound impact it can have on our lives and the lives of those around us. Together, let us embrace self-compassion and work towards building a more empathetic and resilient community.

4

Chapter Three: Decision-Making and Community

Making Decisions for the Greater Good

Decision-making is a complex process that often involves weighing personal desires against the needs of others. In a community setting, it's crucial to consider the broader impact of our choices. This chapter discusses ethical considerations and frameworks for making decisions that benefit the wider community.

At the heart of decision-making for the greater good lies the principle of utilitarianism, which emphasizes the greatest good for the greatest number. However, this approach is not without its challenges. Balancing individual rights and collective well-being requires careful thought and empathy.

One effective framework for ethical decision-making is the "Triple Bottom Line," which considers social, environmental, and economic factors. This holistic approach ensures that decisions are not only profitable but also socially responsible and environmentally sustainable.

Throughout this chapter, we will explore various ethical frameworks and provide practical examples of how they can be applied in community settings. By prioritizing the greater good, we can make decisions that lead to healthier, more harmonious communities.

Inclusive Decision-Making Processes

To create stronger communities, it's crucial to involve diverse voices in decision-making. Inclusive decision-making ensures that the perspectives and needs of all community members are considered, leading to more equitable and effective outcomes. This chapter explores methods for fostering inclusive and participatory decision-making.

Inclusivity begins with creating spaces where everyone feels welcome and valued. This involves actively seeking out and amplifying the voices of marginalized and underrepresented groups. Community meetings, workshops, and focus groups are effective ways to gather input from a diverse range of individuals.

Transparency is another key aspect of inclusive decision-making. By openly sharing information and involving community members in the decision-making process, we build trust and foster a sense of shared ownership. This chapter provides strategies for promoting transparency and accountability within communities.

Inclusive decision-making also involves recognizing and addressing power dynamics. By creating structures that distribute power more evenly, we can ensure that all community members have a say in the decisions that affect their lives. This chapter offers practical tips for fostering a culture of inclusivity and shared leadership.

As we journey through this chapter, we will explore various approaches to inclusive decision-making and highlight examples of communities that have successfully implemented these practices. Together, let us work towards creating more inclusive and equitable communities.

Balancing Individual Needs and Community Goals

Finding the balance between individual autonomy and communal well-being is key to building strong, cohesive communities. This chapter offers insights on navigating this balance and achieving harmony between personal and collective interests.

Individual autonomy is an essential aspect of human dignity and personal fulfillment. However, in a community setting, it's important to recognize that our actions can impact others. Striking the right balance involves respecting individual rights while considering the needs of the wider community.

One approach to achieving this balance is the concept of "relational autonomy," which emphasizes the interconnectedness of individuals within a community. This perspective acknowledges that our choices are influenced by our relationships and the social context in which we live.

Communities can also implement policies and practices that support both individual and collective well-being. For example, creating shared spaces that promote social interaction and collaboration can foster a sense of belonging while respecting individual privacy.

Throughout this chapter, we will explore various strategies for balancing individual and community goals. By finding common ground and working together, we can create communities that honor both personal autonomy and collective well-being.

5

Chapter Four: Building Stronger Communities

The Power of Shared Values

Shared values serve as the foundation of strong communities. When community members are united by common values, they are more likely to work together towards shared goals. This chapter explores how to identify and promote common values that unite community members.

Values are the guiding principles that shape our behavior and decisions. They reflect what is important to us and serve as a compass for our actions. In a community setting, shared values create a sense of solidarity and purpose, fostering a strong sense of belonging.

Identifying shared values involves engaging in open and honest conversations with community members. This process allows individuals to express their beliefs and priorities, helping to uncover common themes and aspirations. Community gatherings, surveys, and focus groups are effective ways to facilitate these discussions.

Promoting shared values also requires intentional efforts to integrate them into the fabric of the community. This can be achieved through community events, education programs, and public declarations of commitment to those values. Celebrating successes and recognizing individuals who embody these values further reinforces their importance.

CHAPTER FOUR: BUILDING STRONGER COMMUNITIES

As we navigate this chapter, we will explore the power of shared values and provide practical strategies for identifying and promoting them within communities. By uniting around common values, we can build stronger, more cohesive communities that thrive on mutual respect and collaboration.

Developing Effective Communication

Open and honest communication is essential for resolving conflicts and building trust within communities. This chapter provides tips and techniques for improving communication and fostering a culture of transparency and understanding.

Effective communication involves not only expressing our thoughts and feelings clearly but also actively listening to others. Active listening requires us to be fully present and attentive, showing empathy and respect for the speaker. By practicing active listening, we create an environment where everyone feels heard and valued.

Nonverbal communication also plays a significant role in building trust and rapport. Our body language, facial expressions, and tone of voice convey important messages that can either strengthen or undermine our words. This chapter offers insights into the impact of nonverbal cues and provides strategies for enhancing our nonverbal communication skills.

Addressing conflicts constructively is another crucial aspect of effective communication. Conflicts are inevitable in any community, but they can be opportunities for growth and understanding. By approaching conflicts with an open mind and a willingness to find common ground, we can resolve issues in a way that strengthens relationships.

Throughout this chapter, we will explore various communication techniques and provide practical exercises to help community members develop their communication skills. By fostering a culture of open and honest communication, we can build stronger, more resilient communities.

Fostering a Culture of Empathy

Empathy is at the heart of strong communities. It allows us to connect with others on a deeper level and fosters a sense of understanding and compassion. In this chapter, we will discuss the importance of cultivating empathy and offer strategies for fostering empathetic interactions within our communities.

Empathy involves putting ourselves in another person's shoes and seeing the world from their perspective. It requires active listening, open-mindedness, and a willingness to understand the experiences and emotions of others. By practicing empathy, we can build stronger, more supportive relationships and create a more inclusive community.

One effective way to cultivate empathy is through storytelling. Sharing our personal stories and listening to the stories of others can bridge divides and foster a sense of shared humanity. This chapter will explore the power of storytelling and provide tips for creating spaces where individuals feel comfortable sharing their experiences.

Another important aspect of fostering empathy is developing our emotional intelligence. This involves recognizing and managing our own emotions, as well as understanding and responding to the emotions of others. By enhancing our emotional intelligence, we can improve our interpersonal interactions and create a more empathetic community.

Throughout this chapter, we will explore various strategies for cultivating empathy, such as active listening exercises, empathy-building workshops, and community storytelling events. By fostering a culture of empathy, we can build stronger, more connected communities where everyone feels valued and understood.

6

Chapter Five: Overcoming Challenges

Addressing Conflicts Within Communities
Conflicts are inevitable in any community, but they can be opportunities for growth and understanding. This chapter explores conflict resolution strategies and the importance of addressing issues constructively to build stronger, more resilient communities.

Effective conflict resolution begins with open and honest communication. By creating a safe space where individuals feel comfortable expressing their concerns, we can address conflicts in a constructive and respectful manner. This chapter provides tips for facilitating open dialogue and fostering a culture of transparency.

Active listening is another key component of conflict resolution. By truly listening to the perspectives and experiences of others, we can gain a deeper understanding of the underlying issues and work towards finding common ground. This chapter offers practical exercises for enhancing our active listening skills.

Mediation and negotiation are also important tools for resolving conflicts. By involving a neutral third party to facilitate discussions and help reach a mutually agreeable solution, we can ensure that all voices are heard and respected. This chapter provides guidance on when and how to use mediation and negotiation effectively.

As we navigate this chapter, we will explore various conflict resolution strategies and provide practical examples of how they can be applied within communities. By addressing conflicts constructively, we can build stronger, more cohesive communities that thrive on mutual respect and understanding.

Resilience in the Face of Adversity

Strong communities are resilient communities. Resilience involves the ability to adapt and thrive in the face of adversity. This chapter examines how communities can build resilience and support each other through difficult times.

Resilience begins with a strong sense of community and social support. By fostering connections and building networks of support, we can create a safety net that helps individuals and communities navigate challenges. This chapter explores the importance of social capital and provides tips for strengthening community bonds.

Another important aspect of resilience is the ability to adapt and innovate. Communities that embrace change and are willing to experiment with new approaches are better equipped to handle adversity. This chapter discusses the role of creativity and innovation in building resilience and provides practical examples of how communities have successfully adapted to challenges.

Self-care and mental health are also crucial components of resilience. By prioritizing our well-being and supporting the well-being of others, we can build a strong foundation for resilience. This chapter offers strategies for promoting mental health and self-care within communities.

Throughout this chapter, we will explore various ways to build resilience, from strengthening social connections to fostering a culture of innovation and self-care. By embracing resilience, we can create stronger, more supportive communities that thrive in the face of adversity.

Sustaining Community Efforts

Long-term success requires sustained effort and commitment. This chapter provides guidance on maintaining momentum and ensuring the longevity of community initiatives.

Sustaining community efforts begins with clear goals and a shared vision. By articulating our objectives and aligning our efforts towards a common purpose, we can maintain focus and drive progress. This chapter offers tips for setting and achieving long-term goals.

Another important aspect of sustaining community efforts is building leadership capacity. By developing strong leaders who are committed to the community's vision, we can ensure that initiatives continue to thrive. This chapter provides strategies for identifying and nurturing community leaders.

Engagement and participation are also key to sustaining community efforts. By creating opportunities for individuals to get involved and contribute, we can build a sense of ownership and commitment. This chapter discusses the importance of engagement and provides practical examples of how to foster participation.

As we navigate this chapter, we will explore various strategies for sustaining community efforts, from setting clear goals to building leadership capacity and fostering engagement. By maintaining momentum and commitment, we can ensure the longevity and success of our community initiatives.

Conclusion

From Me to We: A Vision for the Future

In the final chapter, we envision a future where creativity, self-compassion, and collaborative decision-making are the cornerstones of stronger, more connected communities. We reflect on the journey from "me" to "we" and the potential for collective growth and progress.

The journey from "me" to "we" is not just a shift in mindset but a fundamental transformation that can lead to richer, more fulfilling lives. By embracing creativity, self-compassion, and collaborative decision-making, we can create a future where everyone thrives.

From Me to We: Creativity, Self-Compassion, and Decision-Making for Stronger Communities is a transformative journey into the heart of what makes communities thrive. In this compelling and insightful book, readers will explore the power of shifting from individualism to collectivism, discovering how creativity, self-compassion, and collaborative decision-making can foster stronger, more connected communities.

Divided into five parts, the book delves into the essential elements that contribute to the well-being of both individuals and communities. From harnessing the creative potential of collective efforts to practicing self-compassion and making ethical decisions for the greater good, each chapter offers practical insights and strategies for building a more cohesive and empathetic society.

Throughout the book, readers will find inspiring examples, thought-provoking reflections, and actionable steps to create positive change in their communities. By embracing the principles of creativity, self-compassion, and collaborative decision-making, we can work together to create a future where everyone thrives.

Whether you are a community leader, an advocate for social change, or simply someone who cares about the well-being of others, *From Me to We* provides the tools and inspiration to build stronger, more resilient communities. Join us on this transformative journey and discover the potential for collective growth and progress.

www.ingramcontent.com/pod-product-compliance
Lightning Source LLC
LaVergne TN
LVHW020509080526
838202LV00057B/6259